AF350280

UNDERSTANDING
DREAMS

EBENEZER OSEI BONSU

Mother's Publishing™
We Care For Your Every Book Need

DEDICATION

To my mother, Akua Afriyie, by whose prayers and
godly counsel, I have come thus far.

TABLE OF CONTENTS

INTRODUCTION

DREAMS and their meaning have been trivialised in our generation than any other thing. Its value has been reduced to something insignificant. People no more care whether they dream or not; but the truth is that dreams can hold the keys to our success and failure. Whether this is accepted or rejected, it remains the truth. It's sometimes heart-breaking to hear people exhibiting their ignorance by saying things like the following: *"...but it was just a dream."* Dreaming is as important as seeing with the physical eyes. The only difference is that in dreams, one sees in the spiritual realm while the body is not active. Having your spiritual eyes opened is very important because nothing happens in the physical realm without first happening in the spiritual. The understanding you have of the spiritual realm influences the physical world around you. It is important, therefore, to state emphatically that there is nothing like *"Just a dream"*. You can joke and play with other things about your life but, they shouldn't include dreams. Dreaming is one of the basic channels through which God speaks to people. The position of the Bible regarding dreams is emphatic. **Job 33:14–17:** *"For God speaketh once, yea twice, yet man perceiveth it not. In a dream, in a vision of the night, when deep sleep falleth upon men, in slumberings upon the bed; then he openeth the ears of men, and sealeth their instruction. That he may withdraw man from his purpose, and hide pride from man."*

Unfortunately, people have had serious encounters in dreams that could have led to major breakthroughs in their lives, but they carelessly ignore them and never seek for the needed understanding.

God is not partial when it comes to dreams, unlike the other spiritual gifts. Everyone can dream and everyone must dream. There are spiritual gifts that are exclusively accessible to only those that are born again; however, dreams are made available to everyone without any condition. People dream, whether they are born again or not. The only exception is that being born again opens you up for more detailed spiritual mysteries. In the Bible, Nebuchadnezzar and Pharaoh are examples of the numerous people who had dreams. Though they were Gentile kings and didn't believe in God, God chose to show them great mysteries through dreams, and their dreams eventually came to pass. This tells how basic God has made the act of dreaming. Dreams do not depend on one's spirituality; however, your level of spirituality will determine the kind of dreams you have and what comes out of them. In other words, the kind of dreams you have, and their fulfilment, can be based on your spiritual standing and understanding. Note that there is no need to go about in search for someone to tell you whether you are spiritually strong or not; the kind of dreams you have can do that for you without any second party's intervention. The cue here is that spiritually weak people are normally victims in their dreams. For instance, they are usually defeated when fighting in their dreams. Others will see themselves being chased by evil forces or most times in the cemetery being buried. Any of such dreams must clearly be taken serious, because it points out to one's vulnerability and spiritual level.

I can't count the number of times my life has been spared through dreams. It's an area of my life I will do everything to secure. I have a personal book in which I keep records of my dreams. This gives an idea of the length I will travel to have my dreams interpreted to me. God saves through dreams. Just imagine the state of those who don't regard their dreams, those who don't remember their dreams and those who hardly.

Something happened to me some years ago, which I would want you to learn from. After I completed my SHS education, God gave me a clear word that He was going to give me an opportunity to enrol for University education. While waiting on God to do that, I battled with loads of pressure from family and friends to give up on that idea and go in for a Teacher Education Course instead. I almost gave up on the former when the pressure compounded; However, I dreamt at night and saw myself in a renowned Teacher Education Institution. The whole school was flooded and muddy. Since I couldn't walk through the mud, I took off my shoes to make things easy; yet I couldn't walk across the mud. I immediately woke up and prayed. God then gave me a clear interpretation. He told me that attending a Teacher Education Institution would make me encounter problems I had never encountered before. Thus, I should wait because He would make a way. A few days after the dream, I gained admission to the University.

But for the dream, I would have towed the path God had never intended for my life. This is how many people have made havoc of their lives. Tragedy has befallen several people because they did not heed to the warnings given them through their dreams. Businesses, marriages and families have been shattered simply because some people became adamant to the voice of God that came to them through their dreams.

Chapter One

WHAT ARE DREAMS?

*"And when Saul enquired of the Lord,
the Lord answered him not, neither by dreams,
nor Urim, nor by Prophets."* (1 Samuel 28:15)

A dream is one of the many channels through which God communicates to man to reveal His purposes and intentions. The channels include prophecies, visions, word of knowledge, etc. Each of the channels is distinct by its nature and the way it appears. With regard to dreams, a person is required to fall asleep before seeing or experiencing anything... There is no way someone can dream while walking or is conscious of his environment; when it happens that way it ceases to be a dream; it rather becomes an open vision or perhaps a trance.

A dream is a ladder to the spiritual world, but not until one falls asleep. In dreams, God opens our soulish eye to see in the spiritual realm. God does that because the flesh is a limitation in the spirit world as it can't decode any information there; it takes only the soul or human spirit for a person to dream. In the Bible, Peter could tell the identity of Jesus when the other disciples were fumbling because he could tame his flesh at that instance and draw directly from the spiritual. Jesus immediately knew that Peter had switched from the physical to the spiritual to access that information. He said, *"And Jesus answered and said unto him, Blessed art thou, Simon Barjona: for flesh and blood hath not revealed it unto thee, but my Father which is in heaven."* **(Matthew 16:17)**

That's how dreams operate. Before God speaks to us, He first has to put the flesh to sleep and awaken the soul to reveal whatever He wants to show us. The only time the flesh can be active and yet draw information from the corridors of Heaven is what we call *"Prophetic Gift"* or *"Trance"*. Though there are Prophets who see through dreams, not all dreamers are Prophets.

When there was an agitation between Moses and his brethren (Miriam and Aaron) about who God has called as a Prophet, God came in to draw the line by defining the various means through which He speaks to His people;

Numbers 12:6–8: "And he said, hear now my words: If there be a prophet among you, I the LORD will make myself known unto him in a vision, and will speak unto him in a dream. My servant Moses is not so, who is faithful in all mine house. With him will I speak mouth to mouth, even apparently, and not in dark speeches; and the similitude of the LORD shall he behold: wherefore then were ye not afraid to speak against my servant Moses?

Here, God clarifies his various means of speaking to His Prophets. These are dreams, visions, and face-to-face interactions as if the interlocutors were a man and his friend.

WHY DREAMS?

A dream is the most basic medium God uses to communicate with people. It is basic not in terms of its importance but in terms of its accessibility. Whoever sleeps and slumbers is permitted to dream. Spirits can't dream because they don't sleep. Sleep and slumber are the only requirements needed before one can dream. God is a spirit so He doesn't need to sleep. He made dreams the sole right of humans, who live in the flesh. According to **Psalms 121:4**, *"Behold, he that keepeth Israel shall neither slumber nor sleep".* This clearly means that God doesn't fall in the category of those who dream.

Seeing or hearing spiritual things while awake is not for everyone. Besides, it is not everyone who can hear God's voice while awake. It is the preserve of those who have been endowed with the unique ability or have been called by God to operate in some spiritual offices to do that. On the other hand, anybody at all can dream; no qualifications are required in this regard. Notably, in a bid to know why God chooses to speak to people through dreams, it is important to note that every good teacher or trainer chooses the most appropriate method to teach his followers. There may be several methodologies for teaching but good teachers only select the most appropriate and easy-to-understand methodologies to get the most effective outcome. That's what God does with dreams; the channels of communication are numerous, but He chooses the most basic one to send messages across because of its effectiveness. The soul (the real you) within man becomes more active when the body sleeps. The body somehow limits the soul when it comes to spiritual matters. It is the soul that puts us in a spiritual mode where we can connect with God, who is also a Spirit. Unlike the human body, it is the Human Soul that understands God since it is a spirit. The body is of the earth and, thus, earthly; it is just a container that houses the soul. Unfortunately, many people think everything stops when someone falls asleep. That is not how it is; putting the body to sleep is the awakening of one's soul or spirit. That's why there is a realm called the *"spiritual world"*. Immediately the body sleeps, we are put on a spiritual pedestal, which connects with God. It makes it easier for God to have access to everyone, including those that hate and despise Him. This accounts for why hard-core sinners and Atheists even dream. People may have rejected God in the physical realm; however, when they sleep, their souls submit to His authority. All demons, including Satan, bow to God because He's the head of all spirits.

Moreover, because demons are spirits and also work in the spiritual world, it becomes easy for them to attack a person when the flesh is put to sleep. Every attack of the enemy is against our souls and not the body. When the soul is trapped, the body is automatically trapped. That is why any human being who understands the spiritual world better can let you go after you have insulted him and yet can dangerously attack you spiritually. Whatever happens in the flesh is actually an indication of what is happening in the spiritual world.

Let's point out some facts in David's prayer in **Psalms 124:7:** *"Our soul is escaped as a bird out of the snare of the fowlers: the snare is broken, and we are escaped."*

David's emphasis was on the human soul. He said *"the soul is escaped..."* This brings to mind why the soul is mentioned to have escaped; what about the flesh? Can a physical snare trap a soul? This means the snare in this context is a spiritual snare. The enemy doesn't need your body for anything; all he wants is your soul. Once he gets your soul, he has got your body. This calls for why we must pray intensively for the salvation and the strength of our soul. When your soul is weak, you become vulnerable to a lot of attacks in the spiritual world. The battle against demons is not physical; it is spiritual and so the body becomes irrelevant. Jesus put forth a parable, and this was what he said: *"...the kingdom of heaven is likened unto a man which sowed good seed in his field: BUT WHILE MEN SLEPT, HIS ENEMY CAME and sowed tares among the wheat, and went his way."* **(Matthew 13:24–25)**

Many things happen when men go to sleep. Sleep disconnects us from the physical world and we gain direct access into the spiritual world. That's why while asleep, no man remembers his physical environment; our spiritual eyes get open and God speaks to us. However, the devil also shoots many attacks against our souls. The devil has limited access in the physical world because the world was made for humans and not spirits. It becomes difficult for them to attack from the physical angle; however, in our sleep, we are exposed to their diabolic plans. The scripture says, *"...but while men slept, his enemy came."* Let's note that the enemy didn't come when men were awake but when they slept. The devil is very aware that it is the soul that controls the human body; hence, trapping the soul completely brings the body into subjection and bondage. It explains why they do everything in their power to trap the human soul. God's biggest plan and desire is to reveal the past, present and the future through dreams by communicating to the Human soul. However, through that same act, the devil seeks to destroy and bring man into subjection.

THE TWO GOALS OF EVERY DREAM

God, who made the Heavens and the Earth, is wise. He wouldn't do anything without having a purpose for it. Every creation of God has a purpose for existing. **Proverbs 3:19** says, *"The LORD by wisdom hath founded the earth; by understanding hath he established the heavens."*

This means that everything, including the earth and the heavens, didn't just come into existence. It wasn't haphazardly done. Everything was done by an act of wisdom and understanding. There is nothing that has been created or that exists which has no purpose. It will be an abject denial of wisdom for someone to imagine that there are things that exist without any goal or purpose. Even the unseen exist for a reason. If dreams aren't necessary, as many people have come to believe, God would not have created them as a channel of communicating with human beings. God has some set of goals He tries to achieve with any dream he reveals. He will not open our spiritual eyes in vain if He has no reason for doing so.

Job 33:1 –17: *"For God speaketh once, yea twice, yet man perceiveth it not. In a dream, in a vision of the night, when deep sleep falleth upon men, in slumberings upon the bed; then he openeth the ears of men, and sealeth their instruction, that he may withdraw man from his purpose, and hide pride from man."*

The scripture perfectly reveals how indifferent we sometimes are to the voice of God. The disconnection between God and some people is so wide that they can't decipher between the voice of God and the voice of man. Our ability to connect to God on the things He tells us can deliver us from danger and set us on a path of honour. In dreams, we even see the love of God being demonstrated. He speaks to everyone regardless of race, colour, belief and gender. Armed robbers, murderers, extortionists and Christians alike hear God's voice in dreams. I have seen unbelievers who have had dreams of some impending danger. God speaks through dreams, but unfortunately, people don't get the messages. Sadly, He sometimes repeats particular messages, but we remain blind, ignorant and adamant. The reasons could be that such people simply ignore their dreams, forget their dreams or are spiritually weak. The worst of all is people who claim they don't dream.

From the above scripture, God achieves two goals from every dream we have while asleep. There may be others, but let's dwell on the two goals found in **Job 33:14.**

1. To Redirect the Steps of Man

This is so true and it confirms the words of the Bible in **Proverbs 16:25**: *"There is a way that seemeth right unto a man, but the end thereof are the ways of death."* Sometimes, the carnality in men forces us to take decisions void of understanding that could cost us our lives. Having a good idea is not the same as having God's idea, and not all good ideas lead to breakthroughs; some only drive us into the grave or into troubles. For instance, there are decisions people have taken in the area of marriage, career, traveling, childbirth, etc. which would have landed them in serious trouble, if God had not saved them through dreams. God being a kind Father doesn't want to see any of His creation suffer; thus, He comes in through dreams to reveal to man what could be the end results of any decision taken. Many would have ended up being destroyed and killed, had God not come in to straighten what they had thought would be good for them. Mostly, this comes in the form of warnings to cause us to desist from the things we purpose to do. The story of Abraham and Abimelech shows how God redirects the steps of man through dreams.

Genesis 20:3–6: *"But God came to Abimelech in a dream by night, and said to him, Behold, thou art but a dead man, for the woman which thou hast taken; for she is a man's wife. But Abimelech had not come near her: and he said, Lord, wilt thou slay also a righteous nation? Said he not unto me, she is my sister? and she, even she herself said, He is my brother: in the integrity of my heart and innocency of my hands have I done this. And God said unto him in a dream, Yea, I know that thou didst this in the integrity of thy heart; for I also withheld thee from sinning against me: therefore suffered I thee not to touch her."*

Abraham, for the fear of the people of Gerar, introduced his wife Sarah to King Abimelech as his sister. The people of Gerar were highly immoral and Abraham, who was going to seek refuge there, thought they could kill him and take his wife. Even with that introduction, Abraham still wasn't safe as the king took Sarah to his house to make her one of his wives. The night king Abimelech purposed to have sex with Sarah, God revealed to him in a dream to stop him from doing what he had intended. God prevented him because He didn't want Abimelech to die due to the integrity of his heart.. At that point, God spoke to him through a dream and averted his death. In the same way, many lives have been spared, many evil deeds have been stopped and several negative consequences of people's decisions have been averted through dreams. Therefore, it's dangerous for people to ignore their dreams and fail to pray for interpretation and, thus, miss the opportunity of being delivered from danger.

2. To Rid Man of Pride

God uses dreams as a channel to bring man down from the seat of pride. Sleeping is one the most humbling experiences in life. No man can claim to have avoided sleep, not even for a week. It's an involuntary experience that comes even when we have not invited it. I'm yet to know the strongest person on the face of the earth who has battled with sleep and overcome it. No matter who you claim to be, when the body demands sleep, you must immediately succumb to it.

Immediately the body sleeps, the soul awakes to get connected to the spirit world where God controls all spirits. When we are awake in the body, the soul has limited ability because man controls everything with his freewill; however, when it comes to death and sleep, it is God who holds the authority.

Pride has eaten into the hearts of many people so much that no man in the flesh can tame them. Such people don't allow or expect anyone to talk when they're talking. No one dares them because they think they have what it takes to influence their environment to the detriment of other people. God uses dream to dethrone such people from their prideful seats. Nebuchadnezzar is an example. He is one of the most powerful kings in the history of the world. He could do anything his mind conceived without any consultation with anyone. He brought all the people in his kingdom into subjection and practically demanded worship from them as though he was a god. Although he grew more and more powerful and could control everyone, there was one thing he couldn't control, which is to avoid sleeping. He slept one day and God showed him a dream that would bring him down on his knees in humility.

Daniel 4:4–5: *"I Nebuchadnezzar was at rest in mine house, and flourishing in my palace: I saw a dream which made me afraid, and the thoughts upon my bed and the visions of my head troubled me."*

The dream which no man could interpret except Daniel made King Nebuchadnezzar realise that there was a God ruling in the affairs of men. The interpretation of the dream came to pass right in the presence of everyone immediately Daniel finished making it known. The king turned into an animal and was driven from the midst of men to eat grass for seven years, as the dream portrayed. After that encounter, he threw away his pride and became humble by acknowledging the existence of God.

Daniel 4:33–34: *"The same hour was the thing fulfilled upon Nebuchadnezzar: and he was driven from men, and did eat grass as oxen, and his body was wet with the dew of heaven, till his hairs were grown like eagles' feathers, and his nails like birds' claws. And at the end of the days I Nebuchadnezzar lifted up mine eyes unto heaven, and mine understanding returned unto me, and I blessed the most High, and I praised and honoured him that liveth for ever, whose dominion is an everlasting dominion, and his kingdom is from generation to generation."*

In dreams, God takes pride away from man by showing things that the physical environment may have no control over. Anytime the flesh ceases to offer the help we may need, that is when we become cognisant of supernatural power, which comes from God. There are people who cannot be overcome by anything physical; only a supernatural power can control and overpower them. This is what makes dream critical and important as channel for God to deal with humanity.

Chapter Two

TYPES OF DREAMS

DREAMS vary in their nature and it's important we know them to aid us in our understanding. The nature of my dreams may differ from that of someone else. We are different in the way our thought patterns work. Thus, the way God communicates with me may not necessarily be the same way He communicates with a sibling or friend. He treats everyone differently, depending on how He wants to. Let's find out the various types of dreams found in the Bible.

Numbers 12:7–8: *"My servant Moses is not so, who is faithful in all mine house. With him will I speak mouth to mouth, even apparently, and not in dark speeches; and the similitude of the LORD shall he behold: wherefore then were ye not afraid to speak against my servant Moses?"*

Having established our belief in dreams as one of the diverse channels through which God communicates with us, based on the scripture, let's take a look at two major forms of communication God points out to us. The two are: Dark Speech, which I call Proverbial Speech; and Visible or Apparent Speech, which I also call Direct Speech.

Proverbial or Dark Speech Dreams

Dreams of this nature are not easily understood. It takes people with deep spiritual insight to unravel the meaning. The meaning is hidden in its interpretation. Such dreams mostly contain deep secrets, and joking with them can be very deadly and dangerous.

People wake up confused whenever they have such dreams. It usually takes deep meditation and prayers or those who have been gifted with dreams and their interpretations to make the understanding clear. For example, waking up suddenly after dreaming of a tree can be very disturbing and difficult to understand. This is the nature of dark-speech dreams. God is saying something but your understanding is clouded and unfruitful. It takes deep meditation in the spirit to come out with the meaning. There are several examples of such dreams in the Bible.

Genesis 40:9–12: *"And the chief butler told his dream to Joseph, and said to him, in my dream, behold, a vine was before me; And in the vine were three branches: and it was as though it budded, and her blossoms shot forth; and the clusters thereof brought forth ripe grapes: And Pharaoh's cup was in my hand: and I took the grapes, and pressed them into Pharaoh's cup, and I gave the cup into Pharaoh's hand. And Joseph said unto him, this is the interpretation of it: The three branches are three days."*

Genesis 40:16 –17: *"When the chief baker saw that the interpretation was good, he said unto Joseph, I also was in my dream, and, behold, I had three white baskets on my head: And in the uppermost basket there was of all manner of bakemeats for Pharaoh; and the birds did eat them out of the basket upon my head."*

These were the dreams the co-inmates of Joseph had in prison. They were both disturbed because they knew their dreams meant something deep but had no one to help them with the interpretations. The dreams they had fall within the category of dark or proverbial speech dreams. Both had their meanings hidden. The chief butler saw in his dream a vine with three branches and Pharaoh's cup in his hand, which he handed to Pharaoh. How do you interpret a vine with three branches, if not through the gift of interpretation of dreams or special understanding? The chief baker also dreamt that he was carrying three white baskets on his head and all manner of bake meats for Pharaoh; and he saw birds eating from the baskets on his head. This dream also has no direct meaning; but thankfully, Joseph who was specially gifted with dream interpretation, was there to do the interpretation for them. The interpretation of their dreams manifested within three days.

Added to the above, take your time to read this scripture.

Genesis 41:1–8: *"And it came to pass at the end of two full years, that Pharaoh dreamed: and, behold, he stood by the river. And, behold, there came up out of the river seven well favoured kine and fatfleshed; and they fed in a meadow. And, behold, seven other kine came up after them out of the river, ill favoured and leanfleshed; and stood by the other kine upon the brink of the river. And the ill favoured and leanfleshed kine did eat up the seven well favoured and fat kine. So Pharaoh awoke. And he slept and dreamed the second time: and, behold, seven ears of corn came up upon one stalk, rank and good. And, behold, seven thin ears and blasted with the east wind sprung up after them. And the seven thin ears devoured the seven rank and full ears. And Pharaoh awoke, and, behold, it was a dream. And it came to pass in the morning that his spirit was troubled; and he sent and called for all the magicians of Egypt, and all the wise men thereof: and Pharaoh told them his dream; but there was none that could interpret them unto Pharaoh."*

This dream Pharaoh had couldn't have been interpreted by any ordinary person, except those specially endowed with the interpretation of dreams. The dreams had no direct meaning, so he woke up more confused. He felt he needed help with the interpretation; he needed someone to decode what *"favored kine" and "ill-favored kine"* meant as well as the meaning of the seven thin and full ears of corn. The magicians couldn't interpret them because they had no connection with God, who revealed the dream. It took the same gifted Joseph to bring the dark dreams into light.

This is what dark speech dreams represent. You don't wake up to understand them easily; it takes revelations through prayer and meditation, or people who are gifted to decode such mysteries...

Direct or Apparent Dreams

Direct or apparent dreams are usually understood easily without delay. It has a direct meaning that one can easily understand without any interpreter. The understanding flows with the dream itself. It may not require any spiritual person to decode the meaning. It comes directly and in plain words. For instance, when you dream that you're being chased by a mob into a cemetery, this clearly must tell you that your soul is being sought after by demonic forces.

Again, if you dream that you have been handed a doctor's report with some sort of sickness, without prayer you must know that there is an impending sickness. Both instances are unpleasant situations in the physical realm, so when you dream about it, it must sound an alarm that something is not right somewhere. Like the proverbial dream, the direct dream has several examples in the Bible

Matthew 1:20: *"But while he thought on these things, behold, the angel of the Lord appeared unto him in a dream, saying, Joseph, thou son of David, fear not to take unto thee Mary thy wife: for that which is conceived in her is of the Holy Ghost."*

Joseph being a just man wanted to divorce Mary, the mother of Jesus, privately when he heard that she was with a child. But before he could do that, he saw in a dream an Angel, who told him in plain words: *"Joseph, thou son of David, fear not to take unto thee Mary thy wife: for that which is conceived in her is of the Holy Ghost."* The words Joseph heard from the Angel in the dream, were clear and plain. He needed no prayer or interpreter to understand the message.

Basically, these are the two forms of dreams we have. There could be more from other sources. Whenever you dream, you must know its nature to enable you understand it.

EVERY DREAM HAS A MESSAGE

People attribute their dreams to so many things that they end up overlooking the message or the significance the dream may carry. Many have imbibed some kind of belief that dreams come as a result of hallucination. That is a perception of objects with no reality and usually arises from a disorder of the nervous system or in response to drugs (definition of Hallucination by Merriam Webster). In other words, when someone reacts to a drug or when there is a disorder in one's nervous system, there are definitely going to be images which are not real. Others also think dream come when one overeats, oversleeps or is seriously ill; some people even think dreams come about when someone has his mind clouded with issues. All these demonstrate that people perceive dreams as unreal or unnatural. Whichever way we may look at dreams; nothing changes nothing since the message they carry still hold. Those who think that way may be people who mostly don't get meanings into their dreams or it's possible they even have their spiritual receptacles deadened and don't dream at all.

The fact that you don't understand your dream doesn't nullify the message it carries. Every dream carries a message, whether it is seen as disorganised, unreasonable or forgotten. As already mentioned, dreams point to us the strength of our souls and inform us of past, present and future occurrences. Thus, any dream one dreams has a message it carries. Even forgotten dreams carry messages which have roles to play in people's lives. The fact that you don't understand your dream doesn't mean it's senseless or useless. There is a reason behind what you see when you're asleep. For instance, when you dream about being surrounded by various currencies and wake up to think you were hallucinating or attribute the dream to overeating, you need to reorient your thinking. While some dreams make you happy when you wake up, others make you sad, depressed and afraid. That is actually a sign that you have been hit with a message. The moment you understand that every dream carries a message, which is important, you're on your way to freedom.

THE DANGER OF IGNORED DREAMS

Since every dream carries a message and must be treated with respect and importance, ignoring your dreams does not mean the message is ignored; it still carries the power to manifest, which can be dangerous.

As we may be aware, while God uses certain dreams to reveal the keys to success, He uses others to send warnings of impending danger. Thus, ignoring dreams can be very detrimental to one's life. Undoubtedly, there are many people who are seriously suffering simply because they neglected the dreams they had.

Ignored dreams could be a forgotten dreams, dreams that people see as senseless, and dreams with ignored interpretation. Any of these can be dangerous as the message in it still holds. At times, people dream, and forget their dreams; they only remember them when they come to pass. Let's remember that forgetting a dream does not hinder its manifestation.

Let's now take a look at the interpretation of Pharaoh's dream by Joseph in Genesis.

Genesis 41:25–32: *"And Joseph said unto Pharaoh, the dream of Pharaoh is one: God hath shewed Pharaoh what he is about to do. The seven good kine are seven years; and the seven good ears are seven years: the dream is one. And the seven thin and ill favoured kine that came up after them are seven years; and the seven empty ears blasted with the east wind shall be seven years of famine. This is the thing which I have spoken unto Pharaoh: What God is about to do he sheweth unto Pharaoh. Behold, there come seven years of great plenty throughout all the land of Egypt: And there shall arise after them seven years of famine; and all the plenty shall be forgotten in the land of Egypt; and the famine shall consume the land; And the plenty shall not be known in the land by reason of that* *famine following; for it shall be very grievous. And for that the dream was doubled unto Pharaoh twice; it is because the thing is established by God, and God will shortly bring it to pass."*

Let's note that God is not wicked and heartless to watch things happen to the people made in His image without prior warning or notice. His faithfulness changes not, even though ours fluctuate. Pharaoh was a Gentile king but God still revealed what was going to happen to him. Joseph began by telling the king that God had shown to him what he was about to do. Can we count the number of times that God has shown us what he purposes to do through our dreams? Pharaoh's dream meant seven years of abundance and seven years of grievous famine, not only to Egypt, but across regions. Imagine the danger it could have posed if Pharaoh had carelessly ignored his dream and seen it as just a dream; many people would have died out from starvation. Death, poverty and all kinds of suffering are the dangers that accompany ignored dreams.

If Pharaoh had not sought for the interpretation of his dream, the seven years of great plenty would have been equated to bumper harvest and for that matter they would have eaten and wasted food with no knowledge about the impending famine. It would have been very deadly because generations depended on the dream Pharaoh had. However, the interpretation revealed what they ought to do to save the situation. Not many days later, the dream came to pass as Joseph had interpreted. People travelled from far and near to the country where a king (Pharaoh) handled his dream with seriousness and sought for an interpreter.

Ignoring your dream doesn't mean it won't come to pass. The message in the dream will thrive in all situations to manifest at the appointed time. You can kill a dreamer but not his dream. The brothers of Joseph thought they had discarded the dreamer when they sold him to the Ishmaelite, but many years down the lane, the dream manifested when he was even far from them. God never lies concerning the things He shows us in dreams. They ignored the dream because they thought they had buried the dreamer; little did they know that they had rather pushed him to where the dream would find expression and manifestation.

Many have died and a lot are suffering because they considered their dreams useless. God showed what was going to happen in 14 years to Pharaoh; in the same way, He reveals his purposes to us in dreams to make us more circumspect and forward-looking. There are parents who have seen the destinies of their children in dreams but instead of training the children alongside that dream, they've left them to do what they like. God would not show us something unprofitable and unreasonable. He demands that we become proactive to pursue anything He shows us with utter seriousness.

THE TIMELINE FOR DREAM MANIFESTATION

The years for the manifestation of dreams don't reduce their relevance; it's like sowing a seed. Some seeds can take as many as five years before they sprout; an example is the Chinese bamboo. Some too can germinate within two days after sowing. The years or days it takes the seeds to germinate do not make the seeds irrelevant or less useful.

It is commonly believed that good dreams take forever to come to pass, unlike the bad ones which can take just a short period. This could be true, but it depends on how we look at it. Mostly, the fear with which we feed bad dreams with is stronger than the faith with which we feed good dreams. We easily accept and believe the potency of evil dreams more than the good ones, hence their manifestation. Good dreams are exactly like the blueprint of a mansion. Having a blueprint of a mansion doesn't mean you have a mansion; it takes a lot of work and time to see it as it appears on a paper; however, destroying an already built mansion won't take the number of months used in building it. It can be done within a week without any struggle.

This is exactly how bad and good dreams are like. You may have spent years building yourself, but the devil can use a day to destroy it. A typical example is the life of Job. He acquired so much in his lifetime through the good hand of his God; however, when the devil came in, he used a day to destroy all his lifetime achievements, including his ten children. Imagine the number of years he used to give birth, but the devil within a day destroyed them all. It is also worthy of note that not all bad dreams manifest as quickly as we may imagine; some can take up to a decade before they manifest, just as some good dreams can immediately manifest.

One thing is clear: whether a dream takes a longer or shorter time to manifest, it carries a message, which should be our focus, it's duration notwithstanding. For example, when you dream that you're a billionaire, depending on your level of understanding, that dream can take time to manifest because it may require adequate preparation. When Joseph was 17 years old, he dreamt that his brothers and his parents were bowing to him; it took thirteen good years before the dream came to pass. The brothers sold him and thought they had buried his dreams; however, with time, the dream manifested. Genesis 37:10: "And he told it to his father, and to his brethren: and his father rebuked him, and said unto him, what is this dream that thou hast dreamed? Shall I and thy mother and thy brethren indeed come to bow down ourselves to thee to the earth?"

The dream came to pass after thirteen years of his suffering and preparation. He became a Prime Minister as well as a father to Pharaoh. In addition, all the people were at his beck and call throughout the land of Egypt. His father and brethren even came to Egypt and the dream came to pass right in their presence.

Genesis 50:18: *"And his brethren also went and fell down before his face; and they said, Behold, we be thy servants."*

The message the dream carried never died even after thirteen years. Every good dream God has revealed will come to pass, regardless of the years or months it takes. We always have to focus on pleasing the Lord and watering the message of our dreams with prayers and fasting.

We must not treat any dream as a joke, whether good or bad. It may take years but the message it carries will never die. If it's bad, make sure you pray seriously to kill the message it carries before it comes up for destruction. Ignoring it will only worsen your woes when the day of manifestation comes. Good dreams may take time, but putting on the right spiritual attitude can compress time and bring it into manifestation as quickly as you expect. There are people who always count different currencies in their dreams and keep wondering why it hasn't come to pass. God is showing you the future. It may be that there are conditions you should meet before it comes to pass. Pray and ask God to show you what you must do to get there. The focus shouldn't be on the money alone. When Mary received a message from the Angel about things God had planned to do with her life, she accepted it in good faith.

"And Mary said, Behold the handmaid of the Lord; be it unto me according to thy word. And the angel departed from her." **(Luke 1:38)**

It doesn't matter the years a dream may take, make sure you treat it with urgency and seriousness. Never try to ignore any dream, for the end may be dangerous.

Chapter Three

THE NEW TESTAMENT AND DREAMS

FOR many people, dreams are no longer relevant in our generation. They see dreams as archaic for the New Testament Church. They can't come to terms with why people still dream although there are prophets who tell us the mind of God. To them, the idea of dreaming is an old-fashioned philosophy. However, one thing is certain; the prophetic channel has been one of the most active Ministries from the Old Testament times even to the present day. God has always required a spokesperson to communicate His thoughts in a language people will understand (Amos 3:7). Despite the presence of prophets, God still used the channel of dreams throughout the Old Testament era. Everyone can be a dreamer, but it's not everyone who can be a prophet.

Prophets are specially ordained by God as a mouthpiece to communicate His intentions to people in every generation. However, that is not how dreamers are; whoever lives in the body can dream, so long as the person can sleep. There were prophets, both major and minor per their activities in the Old Testament, yet God made good use of the channel of dreams.

In our modern times, God still relies on the channel of dreams, although there are prophets. As a matter of fact, dreams have become one of the signs of the end time moves of the Spirit of God. In Acts of the Apostles, we see the confirmation of the prophecy Prophet Joel gave concerning the end time church.

Acts 2:16-18: *"But this is that which was spoken by the prophet Joel; And it shall come to pass in the last days, saith God, I will pour out of my Spirit upon all flesh: and your sons and your daughters shall prophesy, and your young men shall see visions, and your old men shall dream dreams: And on my servants and on my handmaidens I will pour out in those days of my Spirit; and they shall prophesy:"*

Visions, prophecies and dreams are spiritual channels through which God makes known His thoughts to all His creation. Prophet Joel's prophecy was specifically about the end time church; how the Spirit of God would be poured out on all flesh. He gave signs that would follow that encounter, of which the channel of dream is one. He mentioned the fact that all age groups, without any exception, would have a feel of the supernatural experience through any of the channels after the outpouring. The phrase *"and your old men shall dream dreams and young men shall see visions"* doesn't mean dreams are solely for old men while visions are solely for young men. What he meant was that in the days of the outpouring, which we are witnesses to, no age group would be left out in any of the channels of revelation. If you don't dream, you can see visions or receive prophecies. It will be dangerous for someone to live and be spiritually blind – without visions, prophecies or dreams – in these last days. Whoever sees with his spiritual eyes has his life safeguarded.

In the New Testament, God saved so many people's lives through dreams and directed them to take some bold steps. An example is Joseph, the husband of Mary, Jesus' mother. Joseph was a fine gentleman who was betrothed to a beautiful young lady called Mary. As the Bible records, before they got married, he saw that Mary was pregnant. While he thought of a secret divorce, he slept and an Angel of the Lord came to clear his doubts in a dream.

Matthew 1:20: *"But while he thought on these things, behold, the angel of the Lord appeared unto him in a dream, saying, Joseph, thou son of David, fear not to take unto thee Mary thy wife: for that which is conceived in her is of the Holy Ghost."*

On other occasions, Jesus' life was spared via dreams. This highlights the role and potency of dreams in the life of man, irrespective of the era. **Matthew 2:13**: *"And when they were departed, behold, the angel of the Lord appeareth to Joseph in a dream, saying, Arise, and take the young child and his mother, and flee into Egypt, and be thou there until I bring thee word: for Herod will seek the young child to destroy him."*

Matthew 2:22: *"But when he heard that Archelaus did reign in Judaea in the room of his father Herod, he was afraid to go thither: notwithstanding, being warned of God in a dream, he turned aside into the parts of Galilee."*

It is noteworthy that even when Jesus became an adult and was fulfilling His purpose on earth, the wife of Pilate came to him while he was ready to pass his verdict on the case of Jesus to tell him of a dream she had. The dream, which terrified her, made her warn her husband to be careful with his judgement.

Matthew 27:19: "When he was set down on the judgment seat, his wife sent unto him, saying, have thou nothing to do with that just man: for I have suffered many things this day in a dream because of him."

Dear friend, God still speaks through dreams. Dreaming will never become old-fashioned. In fact, as mentioned above, it has become an end time movement of the Spirit of God. You can't live in our times and never be involved in any of the spiritual terrains to access information from the spiritual realm. Dreams are as important as prophecies and visions; and we must treat them as such.

CHOOSING AN INTERPRETER

This is one of the most critical stages in issues related to dreams. Not everyone must hear your dream. This is because anyone who understands your dream can manipulate your life; some people can easily understand dreams as soon as you begin to narrate to them. For instance, the brothers of Joseph hated him because they could easily read meaning into the dream he told them.

Genesis 37:5: *"And Joseph dreamed a dream, and he told it his brethren: and they hated him yet the more."*

It was clear from the dream that Joseph was going to be the greatest among them and control them. Even Jacob who was the Father rebuked Joseph at a point because of his dreams. **Genesis 37:10:** *"And he told it to his father, and to his brethren: and his father rebuked him, and said unto him, what is this dream that thou hast dreamed? Shall I and thy mother and thy brethren indeed come to bow down ourselves to thee to the earth?"*

When it comes to dreams, you don't have to trust anyone, not even your family members. Be cautious of the person you would confide in with your dreams; this can generate envy. If Joseph had kept quiet and not disclosed his dreams to his family, he wouldn't have suffered the way he did. These brothers of his, who are related to him by blood, ended up hating and selling him out into slavery. Glory be to God that despite all the obstacles put in his way, the dreams still found expression. Everyone needs an interpreter; but the big issue is whom to choose and how to choose the person. This is a subject every dreamer must seek to know, understand and apply very well. You don't have to ask just anyone at all to interpret your dreams for you. They may have a heart that is different from yours and can manipulate you to destroy you, especially when the dream has something to do with your bright destiny. Let's now take a look at whom to choose to interpret our dreams.

Yourself!

The best person to help interpret your dreams is you; No one can best help interpret your dreams for you than yourself. When God trusts you with a dream, He wants you to trust Him with the interpretation. Most dreamers are interpreters; however, because we don't give ourselves time to seek the face of God, the understanding always eludes us. Joseph and Daniel are known dreamers in the Bible' we know that God also gave them the heart and gift to interpret seemingly difficult dreams. Like Joseph and Daniel, we must know that dreams and their interpretations belong to God and He alone must be consulted before we think of any man. (Genesis 40:8)

There are people who will not even wait to pray about their dreams; immediately they dream, they just consult people to help them with the understanding. Spending time in prayer to seek the face of God concerning a dream is the easiest key for the meaning of a dream. When I dream and do not immediately get the understanding, I pray about it and trust God with the understanding. Within a day or two, the meaning clearly comes to me.

Daniel and his friends went before God to ask for the meaning of a dream they were told by King Nebuchadnezzar.

Daniel 2:17-19: *"Then Daniel went to his house, and made the thing known to Hananiah, Mishael, and Azariah, his companions: That they would desire mercies of the God of heaven concerning this secret; that Daniel and his fellows should not perish with the rest of the wise men of Babylon. Then was the secret revealed unto Daniel in a night vision. Then Daniel blessed the God of heaven."*

There is no secret the Lord doesn't know and there is no secret He can't reveal. Daniel and his friends could have chosen to go and consult mediums, but because they knew that dreams and their interpretations belong to God, they sought Him and truly, they had an answer.

People Who Are Gifted and Called

Deception is on the rise in our generation than any other generation. There are so many self-proclaimed men and women of God who have turned themselves into self-styled prophets and dream interpreters in our world today. This is why we must be careful and avoid choosing anyone anyhow to interpret our dreams for us. Many claim to have written books that interpret dreams, which I have no problem with; however, the problem arises when the interpretations don't indicate the peculiarities of the dreams and various circumstances involved. For instance, if I dream that I'm swimming in a river and another person dreams and that he is crossing a river, the interpretations may vary, depending on our spiritual levels and what God wants to tell us. Interpreting both to mean "impending trouble" because we see ourselves in water could be wrong. However, I have heard such generalised interpretations from many people, which is rather unfortunate. We must be guided by the Spirit of God when it comes to dream interpretation and the sources we must rely on.

Generally, whoever has the Spirit of God and is well matured in handling spiritual matters may be able interpret dreams after seeking God's face in prayer

1 Corinthians 2:10: *"...for the Spirit searcheth all things, yea, the deep things of God."*

It must be noted that being able to interpret dreams goes beyond human understanding. There are people who are gifted to interpret dreams by the Spirit of God. Such people can break down dreams for even children to understand them. Since it's their calling, they don't struggle to come out with the meaning, whether proverbial or direct. For instance, Daniel had that reputation among the Babylonians. **Daniel 5:12**: *"Forasmuch as an excellent spirit, and knowledge, and understanding, interpreting of dreams, and shewing of hard sentences, and dissolving of doubts, were found in the same*

Daniel, whom the king named Belteshazzar: now let Daniel be called, and he will shew the interpretation."

There are called and gifted people around us, who may not necessarily be Prophets or Pastors but can interpret our dreams for us. Know the Spirit someone operates with before you can trust them with your dreams. Not all spirits are from God; some are from the pit of Hell. There are few things we can learn from the life of Joseph and Daniel as Interpreters that can serve as a guide when we are choosing gifted and called people to interpret our dreams.

Carriers of God's Presence

Daniel and Joseph were ordinary people like us, but the only thing that set them apart was the presence of God with them. It was the presence that brought the difference between them and those around them. In choosing men to interpret our dreams, we must see and know the presence they carry before we trust them. How do we know if someone carries the presence of God? The presence of God affects our physical environment and it becomes evident for everyone to see. Potiphar acknowledged the presence of God that was with Joseph the moment he arrived in his house.

Genesis 39:2–3: *"And the LORD was with Joseph, and he was a prosperous man; and he was in the house of his master the*

Egyptian. And his master saw that the LORD was with him, and that the LORD made all that he did to prosper in his hand."

In prison, Joseph still carried the presence of God. All the prisoners knew something unusual had entered. The officer in charge made him the head of everyone, and everyone consulted him because of the presence he carried. Those who carry the presence of God don't make noise about it; their actions are rather enough proof. Allow people who carry the presence of God to interpret your dreams.

Haters of Sin

To choose someone to interpret your dreams, that person must hate sin and eschew evil. God will never reveal his deep secrets to people who entertain and live in sin. For Joseph and Daniel to have been trusted by God with the gift of dream interpretation, it meant that they had attained some level of Holy living. As we are aware, Joseph refused to sleep with his master's wife when she willingly offered herself to him. He made it clear to the woman he would not commit such a great sin against his God. He honoured God in the face of sin, which landed him in prison. God also had to honour him before great men by giving him an understanding heart **(Genesis 39:7–20)**.

Daniel, who was among the captives taken to Babylon, did not only refrain from sin but also avoided delicacies that were offered to idols. He refused to bow to the idols of a foreign land, knowing the accompanying dangerous consequences. **(Daniel 1:8-17)** The attitude of these men, who were known for accurate dream interpretation, was something to be cherished. They avoided everything that was in relation to sin.

People with Prayer as a Lifestyle

Prayer is the fastest way to access information from the spiritual world. The word of God is clear in Jeremiah that *"Call unto me, and I will answer thee, and shew thee great and mighty things, which thou knowest not."* **(Jeremiah 33:3)**

Any time we go before God in prayer, it's a clear indication that we can't do without His help. He immediately answers and begins to show us mysteries which we have no knowledge about. Daniel and Joseph were men of prayer. They could access mysteries ordinary people couldn't see with their eyes. Men of prayer are full of mysteries.

Daniel 2:17–19: *"Then Daniel went to his house, and made the thing known to Hananiah, Mishael, and Azariah, his companions: That they would desire mercies of the God of heaven concerning this secret; that Daniel and his fellows* *should not perish with the rest of the wise men of Babylon. Then was the secret revealed unto Daniel in a night vision. Then Daniel blessed the God of heaven."*

We must get people who can tarry with God in prayer to interpret our dreams for us. They can easily download mysteries from the corridors of Heaven and make them known to us.

People with Records of Accurate Dream Interpretation

Before you tell people your dream, check their records or find out whether they have ever interpreted anyone's dream accurately. He could be a pastor but may lack the gift of dream interpretation. It's not every pastor who can interpret dreams accurately. A pastor can interpret your dream and yet you will not feel convinced about it. It can be clear to you that there's a total disconnection between the dream and the interpretation you're getting. If that happens, know that such a pastor lacks the gift to interpret dreams. Let's read what the chief baker in the bible did before telling Joseph his dream.

Genesis 40:16: *"When the chief baker saw that the interpretation was good, he said unto Joseph, I also was in my dream, and, behold, I had three white baskets on my head."*

The chief baker was perfectly convinced by the interpretation Joseph gave concerning his friend's dream. He saw that it was reasonable and accurate; he didn't need any special gift to be convinced. He just knew by the interpretation that it was good and understandable before he told Joseph of his dream. It took someone's recommendation for Pharaoh to agree and call for Joseph to come from prison to interpret his dreams. The chief butler gave a record of Joseph's accurate dream interpretation and by that, Pharaoh was convinced to call him.

Genesis 41:12–15: *"And there was there with us a young man, an Hebrew, servant to the captain of the guard; and we told him, and he interpreted to us our dreams; to each man according to his dream he did interpret. And it came to pass, as he interpreted to us, so it was; me he restored unto mine office, and him he hanged. Then Pharaoh sent and called Joseph, and they brought him hastily out of the dungeon: and he shaved himself, and changed his raiment, and came in unto Pharaoh. And Pharaoh said unto Joseph, I have dreamed a dream, and there is none that can interpret it: and I have heard say of thee, that thou canst understand a dream to interpret it."*

This implies that Pharaoh would not have called for Joseph if it hadn't been for the testimony the chief butler gave about him. Like Pharaoh did, we must narrate our dreams to people who have a record of accurate dream interpretation; doing otherwise can be very detrimental to our future.

THE ENEMY'S ATTEMPT TO FRUSTRATE DREAMS

THE devil uses several mechanisms to frustrate dreams. Thus, we must know them to save our souls from his grips. The devil battles good dreams to kill the message they carry. Remember that he hates everything of God, so he hates to see God delivering messages to people that he (the devil) thinks don't qualify. Also, he can use that same channel to destroy destinies and frustrate lives. There are several weapons he uses to frustrate dreams; however, we will dwell on only four of them.

The Weapon of Forgetfulness / Blind Spiritual Receptacles

This is actually the principal mechanism the devil uses to trap people. Majority of the people I meet end up forgetting the dreams they have. The devil knows very well that God is merciful and will not withhold the things that happen in the spiritual world to his people; he comes in immediately God sows the seed and snatches it. In His parable of the sower, Jesus states what the devil does with the messages God delivers to His people.

Matthew 13:19: *"When any one heareth the word of the kingdom, and understandeth it not, then cometh the wicked one, and catcheth away that which was sown in his heart. This is he which received seed by the way side."*

It's sad that people wake up with the consciousness of their dreams but forget the dreams. It is very dangerous for us to forget our dreams. Many of the dreams that are forgotten normally carry vital messages. The devil knows that if you are allowed to remember your dreams, you can deliver yourself from what he plans to do against you. For example, someone can dream of an accident or a breakthrough and forgets it immediately. The devil steals it because he knows that if you remember it, you can pray or seek help from somewhere. Nebuchadnezzar dreamt but the devil stole it from him and he couldn't remember it.

Daniel 2:5: *"The king answered and said to the Chaldeans, the thing is gone from me: if ye will not make known unto me the dream, with the interpretation thereof, ye shall be cut in pieces, and your houses shall be made a dunghill."*

The devil stole the dream from Nebuchadnezzar because the dream was about his future greatness and the devil would not want that to come to pass. Daniel went and asked God again to reveal the dream to him and God repeated it. He told the king the meaning.

Daniel 2:37–38: *"Thou, O king, art a king of kings: for the God of heaven hath given thee a kingdom, power, and strength, and glory. And wheresoever the children of men dwell, the beasts of the field and the fowls of the heaven hath he given into thine hand, and hath made thee ruler over them all. Thou art this head of gold."* The devil stole the dream from him because of the message it carried. Let's not forget that there are some people who neither dream nor have access to any of the spiritual channels through which God communicates with man. The devil succeeds in destroying and blinding the spiritual receptacles of such people. They become vulnerable to demonic attacks and lose what God plans to do in their lives.

THE WEAPON OF HUMAN AGENTS

The devil uses human beings to frustrate the dreams of their fellows. A typical example is Joseph and his brothers. He was young, inexperienced and didn't know the motive the brothers had. He thought they had the love he had for them, and that made him share everything with them. The devil entered their hearts to make them kill and bury him together with his dreams. When they saw Joseph coming, they said something.

Genesis 37:19–20: *"And they said one to another, Behold, this dreamer cometh. Come now therefore, and let us slay him, and cast him into some pit, and we will say, some evil beast hath devoured him: and we shall see what will become of his dreams."*

They attacked their own brother physically because of his dreams. If God had not used Reuben, the elder brother, to change their plans, they would have killed him. Some people you confide in with your dreams can attack you in various ways to frustrate you.

The Weapon of Nightmares

Nightmares, according to the Merriam Webster's dictionary, is an evil spirit formerly thought to oppress people during sleep; it is a frightening dream that usually awakens the sleeper. The devil is known to use nightmares to frustrate people's destiny. I know people who dreamt that someone had shot them in a dream and woke up in a pool of blood. Satan assigns his demons to attack people in their dreams to destroy their lives, marriages, pregnancy, etc. He uses nightmares to put fear in us to forget or neglect our good dreams.

The Weapon of Delay

There are people who are on the verge of giving up because of delayed dreams. For example, some ladies and gents even think God lied to them because they dreamt of being wedded, but that has not manifested. It's the devil's attempt to cause our great dreams to delay and tarry as we are made to doubt God's care, ability and faithfulness. Read the next chapter to know what to do to get out of the grips of the devil and his cohorts in this regard.

HOW TO WIN DREAM-RELATED BATTLES

Dreaming is not a child's play as it involves the human soul. Everything that relates to the soul must be given our utmost attention. The human soul controls the faculties of the body, including the heart and mind. The moment the soul departs from the body, the body becomes a total waste; in that case, a person is pronounced dead and irrelevant. The devil has trapped countless souls in their dreams.

The battle in dreams is one of the most important battles we must consciously fight to conquer. It calls for a strategic display of wisdom and power to win. The devil keeps on oppressing people and making life miserable through the weapons he displays in dreams. Many people dream and become confused, not knowing where to go and whom to talk to. Someone confided in me that she saw a strange being coming to sleep with her in her dream. It had been going on for months and she didn't know what to do to stop it. This is clearly an attack against her soul and wellbeing. This can affect everything around her life if she doesn't fight to win. Anything we see in our dreams is from our soulish realm and it shouldn't be taken lightly. To be able to win any battle, be it our ability to understand dreams or to stop the devil from oppressing us in our dreams, you must read what I am about to share very carefully.

Build Your Soul, Not Your Body

Jude 1:20: *"But ye, beloved, building up yourselves on your most holy faith, praying in the Holy Ghost."*

This is where people miss it. The human soul is the real person and not the body. Spending time on the body more than the soul is of less importance. The enemy's warfare is against the human soul and not the body. His main focus is on the soul because he knows when the soul is trapped, the body is trapped also; everything that affects the soul affects the body. In addition, Eternal Life is solely about Soul, not the body.

The devil was not smart when God allowed him to touch everything Job had, including his body. He destroyed Job and everything he had so well that he even covered Job's body with sores. He was ignorant of the fact that as long as his soul was secured and strengthened, the body was going to be restored. The case would have been different if he had been given access to the soul of Job. He is now after our souls and not body.

Psalm 124:7: *"Our soul is escaped as a bird out of the snare of the fowlers..."*

John 6:63: *"It is the spirit that quickeneth; the flesh profiteth nothing: the words that I speak unto you, they are spirit, and they are life."*

It is our human spirit (soul) that needs our attention and not the flesh. The flesh profits nothing in spiritual matters. This is why we must spend quality time, energy and resources on things that build the soul.

When the soul is empowered, it becomes hard for the devil to mess with it. Weak souls are vulnerable in their dreams. Any least thing can destroy them. The more the soul is nourished, the more it succeeds in spiritual matters. There are so many things we can do to strengthen the soul, just as we nourish the body with food and water.

God's Word: Feeding on the word of God consistently and adequately brings about the growth of the soul.

1 Peter 2:2: *"As newborn babes, desire the sincere milk of the word that ye may grow thereby."* The word of God is the food for the soul. Feeding on it constantly empowers the soul to be in a good position to fight its own battles.

Prayer: This is another spiritual food. Praying in the Holy Ghost energizes the soul and enables it to stay awake. We are warned to pray without ceasing, so that the devil will have no occasion to misbehave. **(1 Thessalonians 5:17)**

Fasting: Jesus made fasting part of His ministry. He knew it was very vital for the growth of His soul. He began his ministry with 40 days' fasting to subdue his flesh and make way for His spirit to receive strength. He spoke on the need for fasting throughout His ministry. **(Matthew 6:17 –8, Mark 9:29)**

Doing these as Believers and maintaining a dedicated spiritual life will give us an upper hand over spiritual attackers; we will win spiritual battles.

Fine-tune the Mind for Positivity

The things we do in the physical world can have a great impact on our spiritual life. It is therefore crucial to be watchful of what we profess and how we think. Before the enemy can have control over someone's soul, he makes sure the mind is under his control. The moment you allow negativity and fear to dominate your mind, it's a sign of spiritual weakness and failure.

The enemy capitalizes on that to dominate our souls. He makes sure your mind accepts his projections before he implements them. There are dreams that can make you so fearful. For instance, when you dream that you have been involved in a car accident, you can become scared of vehicles and travelling. That is a seed the devil sows and waits for your mind to accept it. The moment the mind accepts it, he implements it. The mind should be trained to defeat every negative news and thought. Those who have accepted that they will be poor, sick, unemployed, etc. usually have dreams related to their thought patterns. Job said, *"For the thing which I greatly feared is come upon me, and that which I was afraid of is come unto me."* **(Job 3:25)**

Solomon's mind was fine-tuned by his Father in the ways of wisdom and understanding while he grew up **(Proverbs 4:3–5)**. It wasn't surprising that even in his dream he could still ask God for an understanding heart. It was already embedded in his mind.

1 Kings 3:5–9: *"In Gibeon the LORD appeared to Solomon in a dream by night: and God said, Ask what I shall give thee...Give therefore thy servant an understanding heart to judge thy people, that I may discern between good and bad: for who is able to judge this thy so great a people?"*

You will be defeated by the devil when you're already defeated in your mind. This is why it is necessary that we train our minds. Fear and negativity must never be tolerated, as they can expose one to spiritual attacks and defeat.

Have Faith

Faith is a master weapon that defeats the world. Every creature in the world, including Satan, responds to faith. Faith never loses any battle. There is no dream, whether good or bad that can't respond to faith. People who talk in faith, walk in faith and sleep in faith can't ever be defeated by Satan.

1 John 5:4: *"For whatsoever is born of God overcometh the world: and this is the victory that overcometh the world, even our faith."*

Faith is victory, so in the absence of it, one is bound to fail. It overcomes everything in the world. The Elders obtained a good report by faith.

Hebrews 11:32–34: *"And what shall I more say? for the time would fail me to tell of Gedeon, and of Barak, and of Samson, and of Jephthae; of David also, and Samuel, and of the prophets: Who through faith subdued kingdoms, wrought righteousness, obtained promises, stopped the mouths of lions. Quenched the violence of fire, escaped the edge of the sword, out of weakness were made strong, waxed valiant in fight, turned to flight the armies of the aliens."*

The moment faith is released after every bad dream, the devil immediately packs his things and flees. Faith can undo what has been done for years.

In a nutshell, the essence of dreams cannot be overemphasized. Let's keep our spiritual lenses clean and active to enable us see and know what God has for us. Stay strong and alert in the Lord!

ABOUT THE AUTHOR

Ebenezer Osei Bonsu is a prolific writer, a passionate worship leader and a counselor. He obtained a bachelor's degree in Development Education Studies at the University for Development Studies and holds Masters in Theology at the Evergreen Bible College. He serves the body of Christ with his special prophetic and healing grace.

He is the founder of the Students Christian Fellowship on the University campus, a vibrant fellowship that has grown to train several leaders for Ministry. While studying at the University, he was awarded the most influential Student for his extraordinary service towards people of all class.

As a servant leader, he understands where people are and reaches out to them. He is a voice in this generation that encourages, informs and comforts men and women with godly counsel.